爱 ài (EYE): to love

熊猫 xióng māo (sheyong maOW): panda

佛教 Fó jiào (foe JOW): Buddhism

羊 Yáng (yahng): sheep or goat

Scripture quoted from the International Children's Bible®, copyright © 1986, 1988, 1999, 2015 by Tommy Nelson. Used by permission.

ISBN-13: 978-1-7334128-0-3

1 2 3 4 5 6 7 8 9 10 LEO 25 24 23 22 21 20

Printed in China

TALES FROM
FuFu's FOREST
The Power of Love

True Stories
Told by Fictional Characters

By Eugene Bach & Amy Parker

Illustrated by Hopeful

BACK TO
归耶路撒冷
JERUSALEM

"Heeeelp!"

FuFu barely heard the call over the whistle of the teapot. He turned to Yang. "Did you hear—?"

But Yang was already out the door.

"Please! Somebody!" Shan cried just as Yang's head appeared at the top of the pit.

"How in the world . . .?"

"I—I was running to meet you all and, well, I just fell," Shan explained.

FuFu caught up with Yang. He doubled over, looking into the pit, gasping for air. "Are you . . . *gasp* . . . okay . . . *gasp* . . . little friend?"

Yang unwound a rope and lowered it down to Shan.

FuFu looked at Yang. "Wait—where did you get a rope?"

Yang shrugged. "Never know when you're gonna need one."

Shan grimaced as he tried to stand.

"I've got something for that back at the house," Yang said, wrapping an arm around Shan. The three friends slowly made their way to Yang's workshop.

Yang helped Shan into a hammock-like contraption that he hoisted off the ground with a system of weights and pulleys. Just then, Fay flew in. "What's all the commotion about?"

"Our friend here fell in a pit," Yang replied as he pulled some leaves from a plant.

"Poachers!" Fay shook her head. "I haven't seen one of those pits in ages."

"Panda poachers?" Shan asked, wide-eyed. FuFu shivered.

"Yep," Fay answered, "but not anymore. Those old poachers now work to protect the pandas. But I guess that pit never got filled in."

Shan groaned and closed his eyes, trying to shut out the pain.

"Reminds me of a story . . . " Yang began.

"When I lived in Tibet, in the tallest mountains in the world, there was a boy there named Tenzin. His mom was a Buddhist and believed that all of her children would be healthy if she offered one of her healthy children to the temple. So when Tenzin was just a boy, his mother presented him to the head of the monastery, Fó jiào, to be raised as a monk."

"Wait," Shan asked, "he didn't get to live with his family?"

Yang shook his head. "He was raised among monks, there at the temple. As he got older, he studied at the most famous Buddhist monasteries in the world and became one of the most well-known Tibetan Buddhist monks to come from his village."

"One day," Yang continued, "a mysterious visitor came to the monastery and spoke to Tenzin in secret. 'You have family that you've never met,' he told Tenzin. 'They used to live in your home village, but they have since moved to America. And they believe in Jesus Christ.'"

FuFu smiled as he soaked bandages in the pot of steaming leaves.

"Of course that monastery hadn't taught Tenzin anything about this Jesus fellow, and he quickly learned that the teachings of Jesus were strictly forbidden there. So Tenzin set out to learn about Jesus for himself."

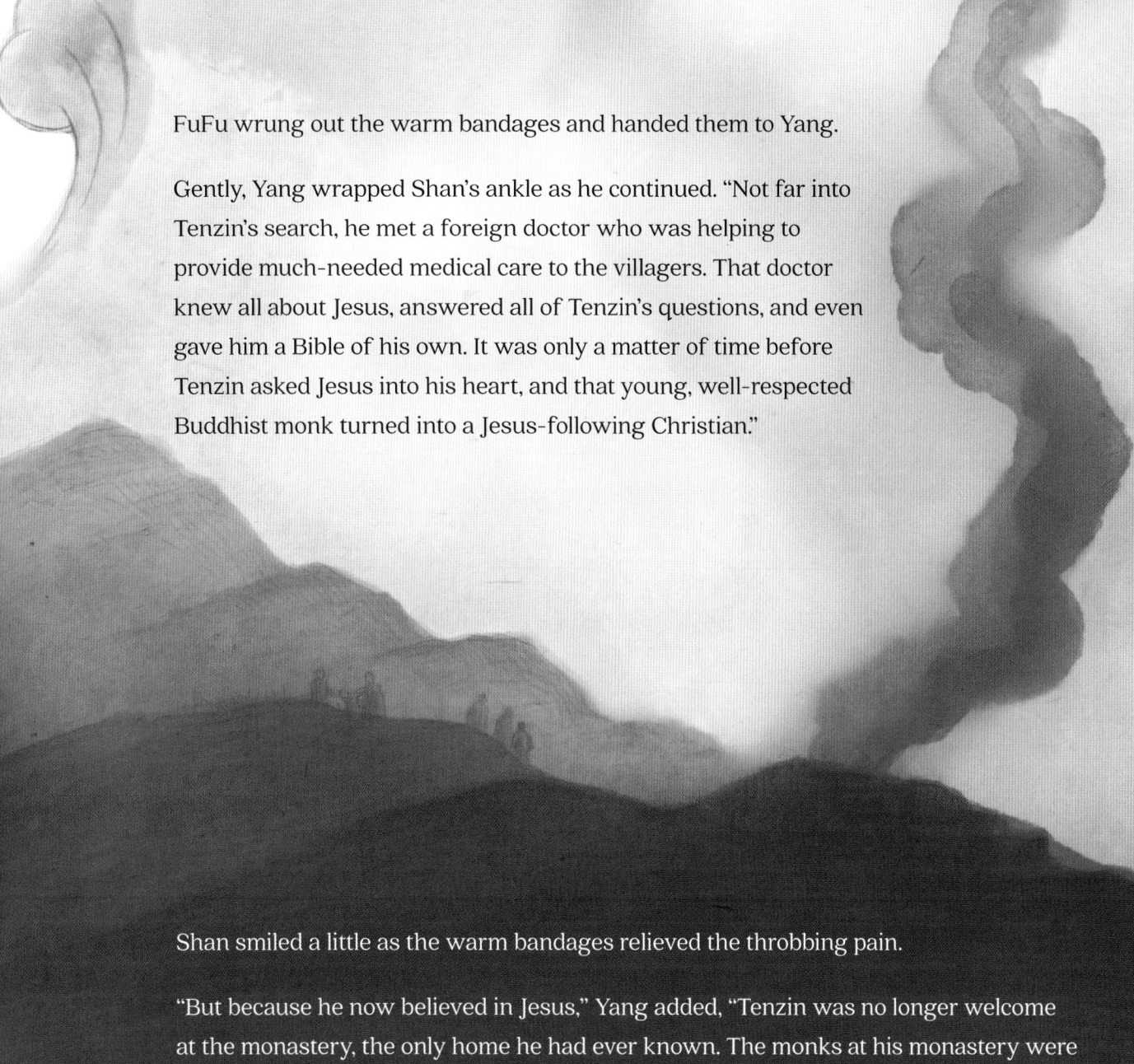

FuFu wrung out the warm bandages and handed them to Yang.

Gently, Yang wrapped Shan's ankle as he continued. "Not far into Tenzin's search, he met a foreign doctor who was helping to provide much-needed medical care to the villagers. That doctor knew all about Jesus, answered all of Tenzin's questions, and even gave him a Bible of his own. It was only a matter of time before Tenzin asked Jesus into his heart, and that young, well-respected Buddhist monk turned into a Jesus-following Christian."

Shan smiled a little as the warm bandages relieved the throbbing pain.

"But because he now believed in Jesus," Yang added, "Tenzin was no longer welcome at the monastery, the only home he had ever known. The monks at his monastery were so angry at Tenzin that they attacked his family, burned down his mother's home, and kidnapped him."

"They took Tenzin back to the monastery, then beat and tortured their new prisoner. But even as the monks were striking him, Tenzin told them about the never-ending love of Jesus.

"One quiet night Tenzin's brother, who was also a monk in the village, snuck into the prison and helped Tenzin to escape. After traveling for what seemed like forever, they stopped, and his brother whispered, 'Tenzin, you should be safe now, but you know that you can never return home. If you do, Fó jiào and the others will kill you.' With that, Tenzin said goodbye to his brother, expecting never to see him again."

"As the years passed, Tenzin heard God whispering to him, the same word every time: *ài, ài, ài*. Tenzin tried to ignore it, but the word would not stop ringing in his ears and in his heart. He knew that *ài* meant 'to love,' and he knew exactly what God was telling him to do: to *ài* his enemies."

FuFu closed his eyes and said with a smile, "'But I tell you, love your enemies. Pray for those who hurt you. If you do this, then you will be true sons of your Father in heaven.' Matthew 5:44—45."

Yang nodded. "God wanted him to love those who hated him, tortured him, and burned down his family home—those who even still wanted to kill him. But Tenzin didn't know how he could ever do what God was asking him to do."

"Still, as time went on, Tenzin thought of all of the villagers who had died because they had no access to medical care. He thought of the Christian friends God had surrounded him with, friends who could help him to build the very clinic his village needed. And all of a sudden, Tenzin knew what he had to do.

"Bravely, Tenzin set out for his home village to begin construction. He knew that he would be risking his life. But he also knew that God was calling him to *ài* his enemies and to help his village."

"One day Fó jiào looked down from the monastery and saw a familiar figure. He couldn't believe it: Tenzin had returned! But the monk's anger soon turned to fear when he saw several other strangers with Tenzin. Tenzin had come back for revenge!

"To his amazement, however, Fó jiào watched as Tenzin and his friends walked past the monastery and got right to work. By the second day, the villagers had joined in to help, and soon the whole village was talking about the new clinic."

"As much as Fó jiào hated Tenzin, he knew that he could never stop him from building the clinic that everyone so desperately needed. As the building grew, the hope and joy of the villagers grew right along with it. Fueled by that hope and joy, the project that was supposed to take several months only took a few weeks.

"To this day in Tenzin's village, countless lives have been saved, and he is still considered a great hero for the way that he loved his enemies, the way that he loved like Jesus."

"So, how's the ankle?" Yang asked.

"What? Oh, I had almost forgotten!" Shan laughed. "You should open up a clinic of your own, Yang."

Yang pointed his empty pipe at Shan's leg. "I think I just did."

FuFu's tea danced in his cup as he chuckled.

WANT TO HEAR MORE ABOUT THE AMAZING TRUE STORY OF TENZIN?

Follow the fascinating story of what causes a highly dedicated Tibetan Buddhist monk to make the radical decision to walk away from the teachings of Buddha and leave his monastery to follow Jesus Christ. *Leaving Buddha* dares to expose the mysterious world of Tibetan Buddhism, with its layered teachings, intricate practices—and troubling secrets. Ultimately, it tells a moving story about the search for truth, the path of enlightenment, and how no one is beyond the reach of a loving God.

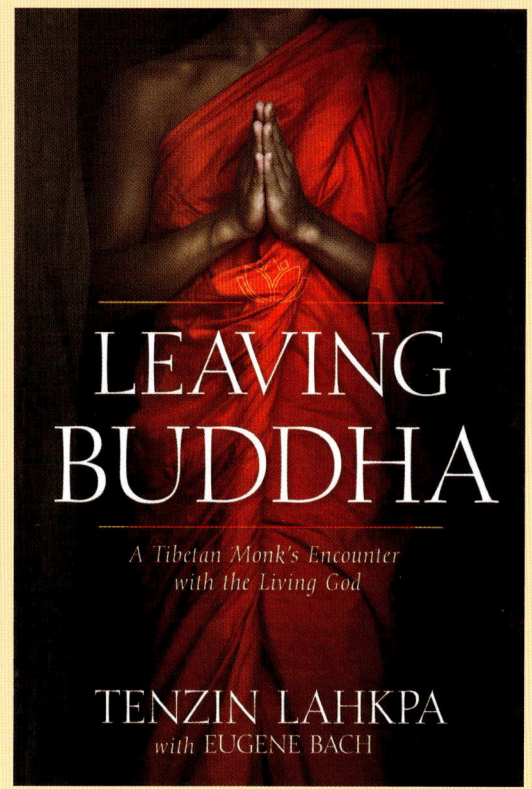

LEAVING BUDDHA

A Tibetan Monk's Encounter with the Living God

TENZIN LAHKPA
with EUGENE BACH

As the three friends worked to fill in that old pit, Shan thought a lot about poachers and pandas, monks and medical clinics, and the amazing power of *ài*.

And when he finally made his way home that night, Shan whispered a prayer for the poachers and the pandas, the monks and the medical clinics, that God would show them all the power of His love.